WORDS TO HELP YOU

BE

POSITIVE

EVERY DAY

Other Titles in This Series:

*Words to Help You
Be a Success*

*Words to Help You Be Happy
in All the Ways That Matter Most*

*Words to Help You Be Strong
Along the Path of Life*

We wish to thank Susan Polis Schutz for permission to reprint the following poems that appear in this publication: "Take the power...." Copyright © 1979 by Continental Publications. And for "Be a Positive Thinker." Copyright © 1986 by Stephen Schutz and Susan Polis Schutz. All rights reserved.

Library of Congress Control Number: 2008904421
ISBN: 978-1-59842-255-9

M and Blue Mountain Press are registered in U.S. Patent and Trademark Office.
Certain trademarks are used under license.

Acknowledgments appear on page 72.

Printed in China.
First Printing: 2008

♻ This book is printed on recycled paper.

This book is printed on fine quality, laid embossed, 80 lb. paper. This paper has been specially produced to be acid free (neutral pH) and contains no groundwood or unbleached pulp. It conforms with the requirements of the American National Standards Institute, Inc., so as to ensure that this book will last and be enjoyed by future generations.

Blue Mountain Arts, Inc.
P.O. Box 4549, Boulder, Colorado 80306

Words to Help You

Be

Positive

Every Day

Edited by Patricia Wayant

Blue Mountain Press™

Boulder, Colorado

*T*he greatest discovery of my generation is that human beings can alter their lives by altering their attitudes.

— *William James*

Introduction

*W*ise words are such wonderful things. Just a few perfect words, spoken or shared at the right time, can change our lives. They can keep us healthy and safe and strong. They can guide us and inspire us. They can teach us how to travel life's path in the best possible way... and avoid some of the problems and pitfalls. They can give us courage. They can give us faith.

Within the pages of this book, you will discover some of the most encouraging and insightful advice you've ever heard. You will be introduced to a number of things you've never read before — but that you'll never forget for as long as you live.

These pearls of wisdom come from a wide variety of remarkable people who share a common message. They believe in being positive, in choosing wisely, and in making each day as rewarding as it can possibly be.

Listen to their conversation, take their messages to heart, and let their words help you be positive... as you continue on your journey through life.

— *Douglas Pagels*

Be Positive Every Day

Life is a mixture of moments —
some happy, some sad,
and most in-between.
Make the most of each day
as it happens.
Don't listen to those whispers of doubt;
ignore any voice that says
you can't do something.
You're worthy,
and you can go as far
as you dare to dream.
Life will lead you
according to your perceptions.
Let your viewpoint be filled with hope,
and keep your eyes focused
on the positive.

— *Barbara J. Hall*

Choose to Look on the Bright Side

Perhaps one of the greatest gifts we have received as human beings is our free will to choose the thoughts we put into our minds. When we finally see our negative thoughts as limited perceptions resulting from our own projections, we can choose to let loving thoughts replace negative ones. When we make this choice, we reaffirm the state of love and happiness that has always been within us, gently guiding us, once again, to freely give and freely receive love.

— *Gerald G. Jampolsky, MD,*
and Diane V. Cirincione

$\mathcal{Y}$ou *have* choice. You can select joy over despair. You can select happiness over tears. You can select action over apathy. You can select growth over stagnation. You can select you. And you can select life. And it's time that people tell you you're not at the mercy of forces greater than yourself. You are, indeed, the *greatest* force for *you*.

— *Leo Buscaglia*

$\mathcal{T}$he way you live your life, the perspective you select, is a choice you make every single day when you wake up. It's yours to decide.

— *Lance Armstrong*

Take Power
over Your Thoughts

You have the power to be happy. It is
a blessing available to each of us, but to
create more joy in our lives, we first have
to become the master of our thoughts,
because emotion always follows thought.
At any given moment our emotions reveal
how we are interpreting what happens in
our lives. When we choose to dwell on
what upsets us, we fuel disempowering
feelings — and that creates the emotional
experience that determines how we react to
our circumstances. The reverse is also true:
Concentrating on the positive not only lifts
our mood but can affect our bodies in a
joyful, life-enhancing way.

— *Andrea Gardiner, PhD*

$\mathcal{T}$ake the power
to choose what you want to do
and do it well
Take the power
to love what you want in life
and love it honestly
Take the power
to control your own life
No one else can do it for you

— *Susan Polis Schutz*

Keep Things in Perspective

*A*gain and again and again, let us be reminded that it is not people or events outside us that cause us to be upset; only our own thoughts and attitudes can hurt us.

— Gerald G. Jampolsky, MD,
and Diane V. Cirincione

*F*ind time in each day to see beauty and love in the world around you. Realize that what you feel you lack in one regard may be more than compensated for in another. What you feel you lack in the present may become one of your strengths in the future. See your future filled with promise and possibility. Learn to view everything as a worthwhile experience.

— Sandra Sturtz Hauss

$\mathcal{T}$he reality of life is that your perceptions — right or wrong — influence everything else you do. When you get a proper perspective of your perceptions, you may be surprised how many other things fall into place.

— *Roger Birkman*

$\mathcal{I}$n every event, in every circumstance, we have a choice of perspective. Faced with difficulty, we can choose between disappointment and curiosity as our mind-set. The choice is ours. Will we focus on what we see as lacking or will we look for the new good that is emerging? In every moment, however perilous or sorrowful it may feel, there is the seed of our greater happiness, greater expansion, and greater abundance.

— *Julia Cameron*

Break the Negative Habit

*W*e can all learn to live jubilantly. We can all learn to alter our attitudes so that we can better realize our dreams. We can all end negative thinking that weighs down our self-esteem and colors our view of life. We can all start down the road to self-improvement at any point in our lives. It does take work, but negative thinking is a habit that can be broken.

— Joan Lunden

*T*he Law of Habit says, *"Any thought or action that you repeat over and over will eventually become a new habit."* When you repeatedly react and respond in a positive way, you take full control over your conscious mind. Soon it becomes automatic and easy to think and act in that manner. By using willpower and repetition, you develop new habits of thinking and acting. By applying this law, you can become a completely positive person and change your life.

— *Brian Tracy*

*I*f you want to make your life happy and worth while... you must begin immediately to train yourself in the habit of thought selection and thought control.

— *Emmet Fox*

Focus on the Possibilities

*L*ook to every day as a day of new beginnings, opening your heart to absolute hope and unlimited potential.

Accept any mistakes you've made; you can't change them anyway. Apply what you've learned and go on. Use these lessons to help you with your other decisions in life.

Embrace the universe. Enjoy the colors of the landscape. Soak in the atmosphere. Smile at the world. Don't allow any self-defeating attitudes to creep into your consciousness. Feel the power of your own acceptance. Put a hopeful spin on every thought you have.

— *Donna Fargo*

$\mathcal{I}$ can do anything. I can be anything. No one ever told me I couldn't. No one ever expressed this idea that I was limited to any one thing, and so I think in terms of what's possible, not impossible.

— *Whoopi Goldberg*

$\mathcal{W}$hen I look to the future, I see more possibilities than limitations.

— *Christopher Reeve*

Expect the Best...

Positive thinking is... a mental attitude that expects good and favorable results. A positive mind anticipates happiness, joy, health, and a successful outcome of every situation and action. Whatever the mind expects, it finds.

— *Remez Sasson*

So expect the best at all times. Never think of the worst. Drop it out of your thought, relegate it. Let there be no thought in your mind that the worst will happen. Avoid entertaining the concept of the worst, for whatever you take into your mind can grow there. Therefore take the best into your mind and only that.

— *Norman Vincent Peale*

...and the Best
Will Come to You

*I*f you expect to be successful, you will
eventually be successful. If you expect to
be happy and popular, you will be happy
and popular. If you expect to be healthy
and prosperous, admired and respected by
the people around you, that is what will
happen.... Always think and talk positively
about the future. Start every morning by
saying: *"I believe something wonderful is going
to happen to me today."* Then, throughout the
day, expect the best.

— *Brian Tracy*

Let Go of the Past

*W*e consume our tomorrows
fretting about our yesterdays.

— *Persius*

*D*well not on the past. Use it to illustrate
a point, then leave it behind. Nothing really
matters except what you do now in this
instant of time. From this moment onward
you can be an entirely different person,
filled with love and understanding, ready
with an outstretched hand, uplifted and
positive in every thought and deed.

— *Eileen Caddy*

When I think of my past, I try to dwell on the good times, the happy moments, and not to be haunted by the bad... To me the gift of life is contained in the command, whatever happens: "Don't let it get you. Just keep on going." Thus... I try to think of the good that I have already experienced and what will still be coming.

— *Rose Kennedy*

Enjoy Today

*W*e cannot change yesterday,
that is quite clear;
nor begin on tomorrow
until it is here.
So all that is left
for you and for me
is to make today
as sweet as can be.

— *Author Unknown*

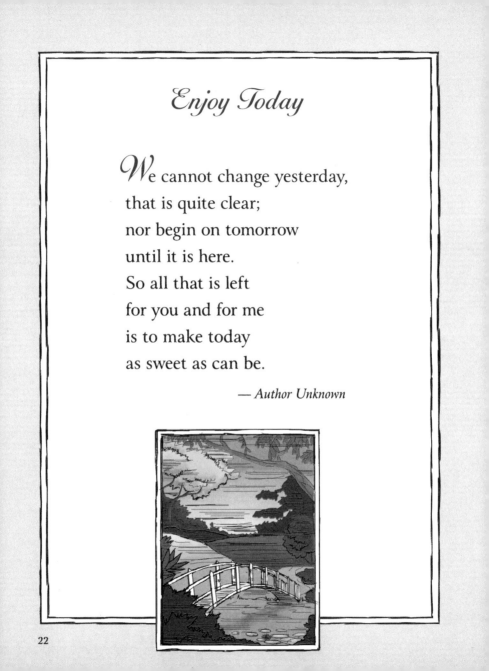

$\mathscr{L}$iving in the present brings the one thing most people spend their lives striving to achieve: peace. Relaxing into the present moment puts you in the mental and physical state of calm, quiet, and tranquility and finally gets us off the here-but-gotta-get-there treadmill. If you are in the moment doing whatever you are doing, then there is no time to examine the gap between your expectation and the reality of how things are, or between where you are and where you think you should be. You are too busy being *in* the moment to *analyze* it and find fault with it.

— *Chérie Carter-Scott, PhD*

$\mathscr{L}$ook with hope to the
horizon of today, for today
is all we truly have.

— *Vickie M. Worsham*

Don't Dwell on Your Troubles

When things aren't working out the best for you... Try to look at what you're going through as a challenge rather than an obstacle, a time to develop patience. Have confidence in yourself, and realize that you can change your attitude even if you can't change the circumstances.

— *Donna Fargo*

$\mathcal{W}$e've all had bad days when stuff kept happening and wondered, "Oh no, what next?" Don't let it throw you off track. Just keep repeating the mantra… It's not what happens to me that's important — it's how I respond to what happens.

— *John Alston and Lloyd Thaxton*

$\mathcal{T}$roubles are only mental; it is the mind that manufactures them, and the mind can gorge them, banish them, abolish them.

— *Mark Twain*

Go Easy on Yourself

Sometimes... when you try to replace a strong negative emotion with more positive thoughts or feelings, the first emotion keeps coming back. This can cause a struggle inside you. In such a situation, another way of dealing with your suffering is to recognize your capacity for being calm, for having understanding, compassion, and peace. This is your true nature.... When you bring to mind these qualities of great compassion and understanding, you acknowledge their presence within you and you will immediately suffer less.

— *Thich Nhat Hanh*

$\mathcal{R}$emember... just as there are clearer skies and brighter days after a hard rain, the stormy weather in your life will also change. Life hurts sometimes, but you will find positive ways to handle disappointment, you will learn valuable lessons, and you will discover strengths to empower you. Life has its seasons, but seasons change, and so can you.

— *Donna Fargo*

Practice Peaceful Thoughts

At intervals during the day practice thinking a carefully selected series of peaceful thoughts. Let mental pictures of the most peaceful scenes you have ever witnessed pass across your mind, as, for example, some beautiful valley filled with the hush of evening time, as the shadows lengthen and the sun sinks to rest. Or recall the silvery light of the moon falling upon rippling waters, or remember the sea washing gently upon soft shores of sand. Such peaceful thought images will work upon your mind as a healing medicine. So now and then during every day allow motion pictures of peace slowly to cross your mind.

— *Norman Vincent Peale*

If you seek peace and love first, if you learn to become mindfully present, you'll find that good things seem to be attracted to you without your even having to specify them. When you think about using the power of your mind in daily life, remember that peace is the most important goal, because thoughts of peace open the heart to love, and they close the mind to fear. Peace and love are the frame of reference through which we discover the mind's true power.

— *Joan and Miroslav Borysenko, PhD*

$\mathcal{W}$e are all given a choice each day. We can react negatively to the demands made on us or we can choose to live abundantly, to transform the negative into the meaningful. Attitude is all. If I do not endow my life and work with meaning, no one will ever be able to do it for me.

— *Sarah Ban Breathnach*

Promise Yourself

Promise yourself to be so strong that nothing can disturb your peace of mind. To talk health, happiness, and prosperity to every person you meet. To make all your friends feel that there is something in them. To look at the sunny side of everything and make your optimism come true. To think only of the best, to work only for the best, and expect only the best. To be just as enthusiastic about the success of others as you are about your own. To forget the mistakes of the past and press on to the greater achievements of the future. To wear a cheerful countenance at all times and give every living creature you meet a smile.... To be too large for worry, too noble for anger, too strong for fear, and too happy to permit the presence of trouble.

— *Christian D. Larson*

Don't Forget to Laugh...

$\mathcal{T}$he next time life gets you down, remember, you have a choice. You can either stay down in the doldrums where there is nothing but more negative feelings, or you can make up your mind to laugh until the doldrums disappear. The choice is up to you. Find a reason to laugh!

— *Les Brown*

$\mathcal{L}$aughter is a form of internal jogging. It moves your internal organs around. It enhances respiration. It is an igniter of great expectations.

— *Norman Cousins*

...and to Smile

*L*ife is never so bad
you can't find something
to smile about.

— *George Foreman*

*T*hink about the good things in life,
like sunshine, holidays, feeling loved,
special friendships, and laughter.
Think about rainbows, butterflies,
and beautiful sunsets and feel loved,
cared about, and accepted. Remember
that in life, although there is some bad
stuff, good things really do happen,
too. And then smile.

— *Maria Mullins*

Be a Positive Thinker

Have confidence in yourself
Have a very strong sense of purpose
Never have excuses for not doing something
Always try your hardest for perfection
Never consider the idea of failing
Work extremely hard toward your goals
Know who you are
Understand your weaknesses
    as well as your strong points
Accept and benefit from criticism
Know when to defend what you are doing
Be creative
Do not be afraid to be a little different
    in finding innovative solutions that
        will enable you to achieve your dreams

— *Susan Polis Schutz*

$\mathcal{Y}$ou are responsible for the thoughts you have in your head at any given time. You have the capacity to think whatever you choose, and virtually all your self-defeating attitudes and behaviors originate in the way you choose to think.

— *Dr. Wayne Dyer*

When It's Hard to Be Positive...

*H*ave hope. Because it works wonders for those who have it. Be optimistic. Because people who expect things to turn out for the best often set the stage to receive a beautiful result.

Count your blessings. Be inspired to climb your ladders and have some nice, long talks with your wishing stars. Be strong and patient, gentle and wise.

Believe in happy endings. Because you are the author of the story of your life.

— *Douglas Pagels*

*H*olding on to old hurts and programmed ideals creates blockages that prevent change and growth. Do you really desire happiness, peace of mind, and serenity? You can have it. Do you desire perfect relationships with your loved ones and creative, stimulating communication in your dealings with others? You can have it. But you have to surrender the old hurts and self-serving thinking.... It's looking at the way you think, examining your feelings and fears. It's facing the most vulnerable and fearful aspects of your person. This takes courage.

— *Suzanne Somers*

*K*nowing in your heart that you are in charge of your destiny can give you the power to overcome obstacles. It's an attitude that carries you through the tough times and that looks at the positives and defies the negatives.

— *Barbara Cage*

Live One Day at a Time

Remember to live just this one day
and not add tomorrow's troubles
　　to today's load.
Remember that every day ends
and brings a new tomorrow
full of exciting new things.
Love what you do,
　　do the best you can.

— Vickie M. Worsham

One day at a time — we have that
ability, through cherishing each
moment and rejoicing in each dream.
We can experience each day anew,
and with this fresh start we have what
it takes to make all our dreams come
true. Each day is new, and living one
day at a time enables us to truly enjoy
life and live it to the fullest.

— *Regina Hill*

Take each day one at a
time, and you'll be amazed
at how your difficulties
manage to become easier.

— *Collin McCarty*

Avoid Negative Talk...

When I join in negative talk there is a price to pay — my inner peace. I will start today to be the best person I can be and realize that gossip and hurtful remarks only hurt me in the end. It is in my own best interest to wish only good for all people. I can start with the next person I speak to.

— *Suzanne Somers*

You have to ignore the naysayers, not let them sabotage you, and go after what is in your heart.

— *Martina Navratilova*

...and Negative Emotions

The elimination of negative emotions is the most important single step you can take toward health, happiness, and personal well-being. Each time you take complete control over your thoughts and feelings, and discipline yourself to keep them positive, the quality of both your inner and outer lives improves. In the absence of negative emotions, your mind automatically fills with the positive emotions that generate feelings of happiness and fulfillment.

— *Brian Tracy*

Change Your Vocabulary

Words to Forget	Words to Remember
I can't	I can
I'll try	I will
I have to	I want to
should have	will do
could have	my goal
someday	today
if only	next time
Yes, but	I understand
problem	opportunity
difficult	challenging
stressed	motivated
worried	interested
impossible	possible
I, me, my	You, your
hate	love

— *Denis Waitley*

$\mathcal{D}$on't even allow yourself to utter the words *I can't*. Delete them from your vocabulary. And every time a negative thought comes into your mind, pluck it out, toss it away, and replace it with a positive idea. This is not easy, but it's doable and necessary if we are to move ourselves and our communities forward.... Moment to moment you must practice staying on the good foot, and in time your positive thinking and optimism will become as natural to you as breathing.

— *Susan L. Taylor*

Watch What You Say
to Yourself

Recognize that the most important conversations are the ones you have with yourself. Whether or not you are aware of it, you have a running conversation with yourself from the time you get up to the time you go to sleep. Your thoughts and ideas are "you talking to you." Have daily conversations with yourself that are supportive and reinforcing. We know the value of talking to people who praise us, reward us, recognize us, are happy to see us, and let us know they genuinely enjoy talking with us. Talk to yourself with those same qualities — silently as well as audibly.

— *Denis Waitley*

$\mathcal{S}$elf-talk is what we say about ourselves to ourselves. You know, that little voice that is our companion on life's journey? Well, that little voice can be a big influence in your life. It just depends on what your voice is saying to you about you. Does your self-talk include congratulations for the outrageously wonderful and fabulous things you've done? Or does your self-talk fill your mind with criticism and nagging at every turn? Tune in. What are you saying to yourself right now? Is it something like "Well, I've never done anything outrageously wonderful and fabulous, so no wonder I never congratulate myself"? If it is, stop! Change what you say to yourself *about* yourself. Undermine the negative messages with positive ones: "I am outrageously wonderful and fabulous." Soon you will be — if you aren't already!

— *Cheri K. Erdman*

The Worriers' Guild

Today there is a meeting of the
Worriers' Guild,
and I'll be there.
The problems of Earth are
   to be discussed
   at length
   end to end
   for five days
   end to end
   with 1100 countries represented
   all with an equal voice
   some wearing turbans and smocks
   and all the men will speak
   and the women
   with or without notes
   in 38 languages
   and nine different species of logic.

Outside in the autumn
  the squirrels will be
  chattering and scampering
  directionless throughout the town
  because
they aren't organized yet.

        — Philip F. Deaver

Open Up to Optimism

*T*here is one thing which
gives radiance to everything:
It is the idea of something
around the corner.

— *G. K. Chesterton*

I believe that we form our own lives,
that we create our own reality, and
that everything works out for the best.
I know I drive some people crazy with
what seems to be ridiculous optimism,
but it has always worked out for me.

— *Jim Henson*

*R*eal optimism is aware of problems
but recognizes the solutions, knows
about difficulties but believes they can
be overcome, sees the negatives but
accentuates the positives, is exposed
to the worst but expects the best, has
reason to complain but chooses to smile.

— *William Arthur Ward*

*O*ptimism is a happiness magnet. If you
stay positive, good things and good people
will be drawn to you. Everyone wants to
be around somebody who can bring cheer
and humor to any situation, and optimistic
people have a way of finding good things
around every corner. I've seen it happen over
and over again. Unfortunately, the opposite
is also true. A negative attitude is like an
advertisement for unhappiness.

— *Mary Lou Retton*

Be Forgiving

If you are generally a realistic, positive person as you move through life, you'll probably be comfortable with the people and circumstances you encounter. You'll be flexible and open to life and whatever it decides to bring to you. Have the ability to let go and find forgiveness — you'll take back laughter and lightness into your daily life.

Dwell on the positive... you gain power.

Cling to the negative, all you'll have is a headache.

— *Joan Lunden*

To forgive is the highest, most beautiful form of love. In return, you will receive untold peace and happiness.

— *Robert Muller*

*H*arboring grudges and hostility against anyone including yourself tends to attract more circumstances to be upset about. Practice forgiving somebody everyday for any real or imagined transgressions. The better you become at forgiveness, the more positive you can become as a human being.

— *Tommy Newberry*

Improve Your Health...

*Y*ou can make yourself ill with your thoughts and by the same token you can make yourself well by the use of a different and healing type of thought. Think one way and you attract the conditions which that type of thinking indicates. Think another way and you can create an entirely different set of conditions. Conditions are created by thoughts far more powerfully than conditions create thoughts.

— *Norman Vincent Peale*

*D*rag your thoughts away
from your troubles... it's the
healthiest thing a body can do.

— *Mark Twain*

...Improve Your Life

We have the ability, right, and power to create whatever we want in our lives. All we have to do is see it. We can choose to see the unlimited possibilities, rich opportunities, and uncharted waters. We can choose to see that doing what we want with ease, having what we want with joy, and being where we want can be used for projection and perception. When we use our eyes to project what we want into the world, we send forth the creative power of the soul's force. When we use positive perception to interpret what we see, we avoid falling prey to doom and gloom. If we can look beyond today, its challenges and obstacles, we can create a better tomorrow. If we can see, it must come to be. That is the law.

— *Iyanla Vanzant*

Look for the Good in All Situations

It doesn't take any more time to think in a way that makes your life better than it does to think in a way that makes your life miserable. People whose inner spirit spills over into their lives in the real world look for the good, and their days flow smoothly most of the time. When you ask how they are and they tell you they're fine, they mean it. This isn't the kind of positive thinking that's regimented and enforced, but simply a nod to the good given often enough that it becomes natural.

— *Victoria Moran*

$\mathcal{T}$he truth is, we see in life what we want to see. If you search for ugliness you'll find plenty of it. If you want to find fault with other people, your career, or the world in general, you'll certainly be able to do so. But the opposite is also true. If you look for the extraordinary in the ordinary, you can train yourself to see it.

— *Richard Carlson, PhD*

Always Have Hope

One thing I had learned over the years:
hope is precious, and there's no reason to
give it up until you absolutely have to.

— *Elizabeth Edwards*

Never stop wishing on stars,
    dreaming on clouds,
    looking for four-leaf clovers,
    admiring rainbows,
    watching butterflies,
    hoping for magic,
    expecting the miraculous,
    believing in the serendipitous wonders
    and great coincidences of life.

— *Susan Skog*

*R*efuse to dwell on the mistakes
　　or disappointments
that are sometimes a part of life;
instead learn how you can
　　make things better.
Be optimistic.
Be energetic and positive
　　about the things you do,
and always hope for the best.

　　　　　　　　　　　— *Ben Daniels*

*W*hen you think about it, what
other choice is there but to hope?

　　　　　　　　　　　— *Lance Armstrong*

Believe in the Power of a Positive Attitude

Believe that:
* You can do it.
* You're in control of your life.
* Your life is meaningful.
* Your life is manageable.
* Life is great.
* People are basically good.
* If things are bad now, they'll get better.
* You *can* make a difference.

> — *Arnold Fox, MD,*
> *and Barry Fox, PhD*

$\mathcal{E}$verything we think affects our spirit, our attitude, and our ability to participate in life. In fact, it has often been said that *what we become is what we think about most of the time.*

— *Joan Lunden*

$\mathcal{T}$o have the belief that every experience, without exception, is a positive lesson in our lives, from which we can learn and grow, itself generates our willingness to receive all of life's experiences. We can then create positive results from all that life offers us, accepting each lesson with gratitude even before we know what the benefits might be. While our willingness opens us up to the opportunity for growth, our gratitude opens us up to receiving it.

— *Gerald G. Jampolsky, MD, and Diane V. Cirincione*

Surround Yourself
with Positive People

*Y*ou must become the guardian of your
thoughts and actions. It's imperative
that you surround yourself with positive
people — those who affirm you and
show by their words and deeds that they
like you and believe in your dreams.

— *Susan L. Taylor*

*T*here is little difference in people,
but that little difference makes a
big difference. That little difference
is attitude. The big difference is
whether it is positive or negative.

— *W. Clement Stone*

The positive people that you meet change your life because they are able to model for you the mindset and habits that you need and are lacking in your life. They effectively do both because they challenge you to think differently and put into action what you have learned in order to make powerful changes in your life.

— *Michael Murphy*

Guarantee your peace of mind, contentment, faith, and strength, as well as the constant ability to find joy in all the things that sometimes go unnoticed. Find moments to connect with other individuals who are full of smiles and hugs to give away and stories and laughter to share.

— *Barbara Cage*

Start Each Day Anew

Think of this when you wake up each morning. You have a fresh start, a clean slate, and a chance to work on things you want to improve while enjoying the opportunities life offers.

You never know what lies ahead, but you do have control over today's decisions and choices — to shape your path and influence your tomorrows.

Each day is a bright, new beginning to embrace and enjoy. Appreciate all its blessings.

— *Debbie Burton-Peddle*

I wake up every day with the intention to be loving and happy and the best I can be.

— *Goldie Hawn*

I believe in taking a positive attitude toward the world, toward people, and toward my work.... I try to think of myself as a part of all of us — all mankind and all life. I find it's not easy to keep these lofty thoughts in mind as the day goes by, but it certainly helps me a great deal to start out this way.

— *Jim Henson*

Leave Good Footprints

*L*ife is a precious journey we all take. Each decision we make leaves an indelible footprint, for good or bad, success or failure, happiness or sorrow. So walk carefully and with much thought, for your footprints will follow you wherever you go.

Make good footprints. Walk in love. Reach out in kindness. Speak peace. Harm no one. Be a light for goodness. Live in truth. Spread hope. Embrace others. Build bridges. Be a friend to all. Show compassion. Champion respect. Give your best. Do what is right. Make a difference. (Everyone can!)

Live your life in such a thoughtful and positive way that when you or others look back on the landscape of your life, you will feel proud of the footprints you have left behind.

Good footprints will not only allow you to live well, happy, and at peace. They will make this world — which sometimes seems so crazy — a better place because it was graced by your presence, blessed by your spirit, and gifted by your bright legacy.

Wherever you go in this life... leave good footprints behind you.

— *Nancye Sims*

Change Your Thoughts...

*T*he good news is that you can have everything you want in life, you can be anything you want to be, you can do everything you want to do, and there is only one condition: you must make a solid commitment to yourself to change your thoughts....

Positive thoughts... lead directly to positive results in everything you do.... It is your attitude that controls your very destiny, for good or for bad.

— *Thomas W. Foster*

...Change Your Life

I am convinced that attitude is the key to success or failure in almost any of life's endeavors. Your attitude — your perspective, your outlook, how you feel about yourself, how you feel about other people — determines your priorities, your actions, your values. Your attitude determines how you interact with other people and how you interact with yourself.

— *Caroline Warner*

*T*hought is the great builder in human life: it is the determining factor. Continually think thoughts that are good, and your life will show forth in goodness.... Think thoughts of love, and you will love and will be loved.

— *Ralph Waldo Trine*

Make Every Day a Great Day to Be Alive

Wake up every day in a good mood with a smile for the world and a sunny, easy, and positive attitude, no matter what the weather is like or whatever the circumstances. As you go about your day, take the time to celebrate yourself and the lives of those you care about, and realize how important you are to all those who know you. Let your last thought in the evening be one of gratitude for such a great day.

— *Donna Fargo*

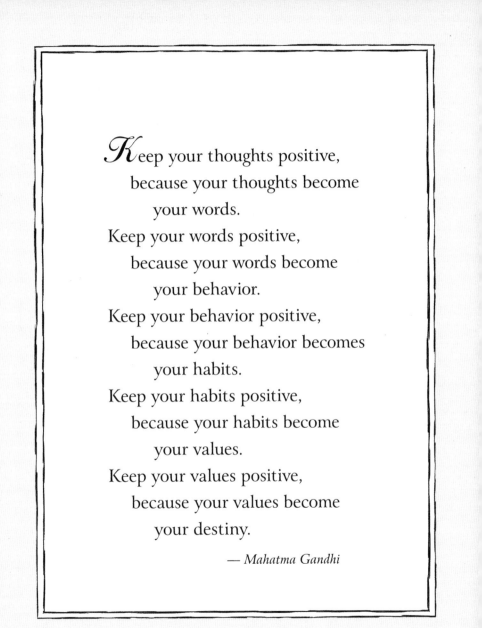

$\mathcal{K}$eep your thoughts positive,
    because your thoughts become
        your words.
Keep your words positive,
    because your words become
        your behavior.
Keep your behavior positive,
    because your behavior becomes
        your habits.
Keep your habits positive,
    because your habits become
        your values.
Keep your values positive,
    because your values become
        your destiny.

— *Mahatma Gandhi*

May You Always Have Positive Thoughts

May each new day of your life bring you fresh hopes for tomorrow and feelings of excitement, joy, and a wonderful sense of expectation.

May you remember the good times and forget the sorrow and pain, for the good times will remind you of how special your life has been.

May you always feel secure and loved and know you are the best.

May you experience all the good things in life — the happiness of realizing your dreams, the joy of feeling worthwhile, and the satisfaction of knowing you've succeeded.

May you find warmth in others, expressions of love and kindness, smiles that encourage you, and friends who are loyal and honest.

May you realize the importance of patience and accept others for what they are. With understanding and love, you'll find the good in every heart.

Above all, may you always have positive thoughts.

— *Regina Hill*

ACKNOWLEDGMENTS

We gratefully acknowledge the permission granted by the following authors, publishers, and authors' representatives to reprint poems or excerpts from their publications.

Barbara J. Hall for "Life is a mixture of moments...." Copyright © 2008 by Barbara J. Hall. All rights reserved.

Bantam Books, a division of Random House, Inc., for "Perhaps one of the greatest gifts...," "Again and again and again...," and "To have the belief..." from LOVE IS THE ANSWER: CREATING POSITIVE RELATIONSHIPS by Gerald G. Jampolsky, MD, and Diane V. Cirincione. Copyright © 1990 by Gerald G. Jampolsky, MD, and Diane V. Cirincione. All rights reserved.

SLACK Incorporated for "You have a choice" from LIVING, LOVING & LEARNING by Leo Buscaglia, PhD, published by Ballantine Books. Copyright © 1982 by Leo F. Buscaglia, Inc. All rights reserved.

Broadway Books, a division of Random House, Inc., for "The way you live your life..." from EVERY SECOND COUNTS by Lance Armstrong. Copyright © 2003 by Lance Armstrong. All rights reserved. And for "Living in the present..." from IF LIFE IS A GAME, THESE ARE THE RULES by Chérie Carter-Scott. Copyright © 1998 by Chérie Carter-Scott, PhD. All rights reserved. And for "Optimism is a happiness magnet" from MARY LOU RETTON'S GATEWAY TO HAPPINESS by Mary Lou Retton. Copyright © 2000 by MLR Entertainment, Inc. All rights reserved. And for "One thing I had learned..." from SAVING GRACES: FINDING SOLACE AND STRENGTH FROM FRIENDS AND STRANGERS by Elizabeth Edwards. Copyright © 2006 by Elizabeth Edwards. All rights reserved.

Andrea Gardiner, PhD, for "You have the power to be happy" from "Don't Worry, Be Happy" (Essence: April 2008). Copyright © 2008 by Andrea Gardiner. All rights reserved.

Birkman International, www.birkman.com, for "The reality of life is..." by Roger Birkman. Copyright © 2008 by Roger Birkman. All rights reserved.

Jeremy P. Tarcher, a division of Penguin Group (USA), Inc., for "In every sense..." from BLESSINGS: PRAYERS AND DECLARATIONS FOR A HEARTFUL LIFE by Julia Cameron. Copyright © 1998 by Julia Cameron. All rights reserved.

McGraw-Hill for "We can all learn to live jubilantly," "If you are generally...," and "Everything we think..." from WAKE-UP CALLS by Joan Lunden. Copyright © 2001 by New Life Entertainment, Inc. All rights reserved.

John Wiley & Sons, Inc., for "The Law of Habit says...," "If you expect to be...," and "The elimination of negative..." from CHANGE YOUR THINKING CHANGE YOUR LIFE by Brian Tracy. Copyright © 2003 by Brian Tracy. All rights reserved.

PrimaDonna Entertainment Corp. for "Look to every day as...," "When things aren't working out...," "Remember... just as there are clearer skies...," and "Wake up every day..." by Donna Fargo. Copyright © 1997 by PrimaDonna Entertainment Corp. All rights reserved.

William Morrow, a division of HarperCollins Publishers, for "I can do anything" from BOOK by Whoopi Goldberg. Copyright © 1997 by Whoopi Goldberg. All rights reserved.

Ballantine Books, a division of Random House, Inc., for "When I look..." from STILL ME by Christopher Reeve. Copyright © 1998 by Cambria Productions, Inc. All rights reserved.

Remez Sasson, www.SuccessConsciousness.com, for "Positive thinking is..." Copyright © 2008 by Remez Sasson. All rights reserved.

Fireside, a division of Simon & Schuster Adult Publishing Group, for "So expect the best at all times," "At intervals during the day...," and "You can make yourself..." from THE POWER OF POSITIVE THINKING by Norman Vincent Peale. Copyright © 1952 by Prentice-Hall, Inc. All rights reserved. And for "We have the ability..." from ACTS OF FAITH: DAILY MEDITATIONS FOR PEOPLE OF COLOR by Iyanla Vanzant. Copyright © 1993 by Iyanla Vanzant. All rights reserved.

Findhorn Press for "Dwell not on the past" from GOD SPOKE TO ME by Eileen Caddy. Copyright © 1992 by Eileen Caddy. All rights reserved.

Doubleday, a division of Random House, Inc., for "When I think of my past..." from TIMES TO REMEMBER by Rose Fitzgerald Kennedy. Copyright © 1974 by the Joseph P. Kennedy, Jr. Foundation. All rights reserved. And for "Don't even allow yourself to utter...," "There will never be...," and "You must become..." from LESSONS IN LIVING by Susan L. Taylor. Copyright © 1995 by Susan L. Taylor. All rights reserved.

John Wiley & Sons, Inc., for "We've all had bad days..." from STUFF HAPPENS by John Alston and Lloyd Thaxton. Copyright © 2003 by John Alston and Lloyd Thaxton. All rights reserved.

Free Press, a division of Simon & Schuster Adult Publishing Group, for "Sometimes... when you try to replace..." from CREATING TRUE PEACE: ENDING VIOLENCE IN YOURSELF, YOUR FAMILY, YOUR COMMUNITY, AND THE WORLD by Thich Nhat Hanh. Copyright © 2003 by The Venerable Thich Nhat Hanh. All rights reserved.

Hay House, Inc for "If you seek peace and love..." from THE POWER OF THE MIND TO HEAL by Joan Borysenko, PhD, and Miroslav Borysenko, PhD. Copyright © 1994 by Joan Borysenko, PhD, and Miroslav Borysenko. All rights reserved. And for "Believe that..." from BEYOND POSITIVE THINKING: PUTTING YOUR THOUGHTS INTO ACTION by Arnold Fox, MD, and Barry Fox, PhD. Copyright © 1991 by Arnold Fox, MD, and Barry Fox, PhD. All rights reserved.

Grand Central Publishing for "We are all given a choice..." from SIMPLE ABUNDANCE by Sarah Ban Breathnach. Copyright © 1996 by Sarah Ban Breathnach. Reprinted by permission of Grand Central Publishing. All rights reserved.

Les Brown Enterprises for "The next time life gets..." from UP THOUGHTS FOR DOWN TIMES by Les Brown. Copyright © 2003 by Les Brown Enterprises. All rights reserved.

W. W. Norton & Company, Inc., for "Laughter is a form of..." from HUMAN OPTIONS. Copyright © 1981 by Norman Cousins. All rights reserved.

Simon & Schuster Adult Publishing Group for "Life is never so bad..." from GEORGE FOREMAN'S GUIDE TO LIFE by George Foreman. Copyright © 2002 by George Foreman. All rights reserved. And for "You are responsible..." from THE SKY'S THE LIMIT by Dr. Wayne Dyer. Copyright © 1980 by Wayne W. Dyer. All rights reserved.

Crown Books, a division of Random House, Inc., for "Holding on to old hurts..." and "When I join in..." from 365 WAYS TO CHANGE YOUR LIFE by Suzanne Somers. Copyright © 1999 by Suzanne Somers. All rights reserved.

Rodale, Inc., Emmaus, PA, 18098, www.rodalestore.com, for "You have to ignore..." from SHAPE YOUR SELF by Martina Navratilova. Copyright © 2006 by Martina Navratilova. All rights reserved. And for "Appreciating life..." from WHAT HAPPY PEOPLE KNOW: HOW THE NEW SCIENCE OF HAPPINESS CAN CHANGE YOUR LIFE FOR THE BETTER by Dan Baker, PhD, and Cameron Stauth. Copyright © 2003 by Dan Baker, PhD, and Cameron Stauth. All rights reserved.

Pathfinder Publishing for "The good news is..." from YOUR MIND POWER UNLEASHED by Thomas W. Foster. Copyright © 2001 by Thomas W. Foster. All rights reserved.

Revell, a division of Baker Book House, for "Words to Forget" from THE SEEDS OF GREATNESS by Denis Waitley. Copyright © 1984 by Denis Waitley. All rights reserved.

Denis Waitley, www.deniswaitley.com, for "Recognize that the most important..." from "Confidence – You Only Sell You." Copyright © 2005 by Denis Waitley. All rights reserved.

Gurze Books for "Self-talk is what we say..." from LIVE LARGE by Cheri K. Erdman. Copyright © 1997 by Cheri K. Erdman. All rights reserved.

Anhinga Press for "The Worriers' Guild" from HOW MEN PRAY by Philip F. Deaver. Copyright © 2005 by Philip K. Deaver. All rights reserved.

Hyperion for "I believe that we form..." and "I believe in taking..." from IT'S NOT EASY BEING GREEN: AND OTHER THINGS TO CONSIDER by Jim Henson, The Muppets, and Friends. Copyright © 2005 by Cheryl Henson. Reprinted by permission. All rights reserved. And for "The truth is, we see in life..." from DON'T SWEAT THE SMALL STUFF... AND IT'S ALL SMALL STUFF by Richard Carlson, PhD. Copyright © 1997 by Richard Carlson, PhD. Reprinted by permission. All rights reserved.

Robert Muller, former UN Assistant Secretary General, author of MOST OF ALL THEY TAUGHT ME HAPPINESS, www.robertmuller.org, for "To forgive is the highest..." from "Decide to Forgive." Copyright © 1996 by Robert Muller. All rights reserved.

The 1% Club, www.1percentclub.com, for "The positive people that you meet..." from "Cultivate a Positive Attitude!" by Tommy Newberry. Copyright © 2008 by The 1% Club and Tommy Newberry. All rights reserved.

HarperCollins Publishers for "It doesn't take any more time..." from CREATING A CHARMED LIFE by Victoria Moran. Copyright © 1999 by Victoria Moran. All rights reserved.

Susan Skog for "Never stop wishing on stars...." Copyright © 2008 by Susan Skog. All rights reserved.

Berkley Books, a division of Penguin Group (USA), Inc., for "More than you think about it..." from IT'S NOT ABOUT THE BIKE by Lance Armstrong with Sally Jenkins. Copyright © 2000, 2001 by Lance Armstrong. All rights reserved.

Michael Murphy, www.PositiveAttitudes.com, for "The positive people that you meet..." from INSTANT SUCCESS THROUGH POWERFUL ATTITUDES. Copyright © 2006 by Michael D. Murphy. All rights reserved.

Debbie Burton-Peddle for "Treat Every Day As a New Day." Copyright © 2008 by Debbie Burton-Peddle. All rights reserved.

G.P. Putnam's Sons, a division of Penguin Group (USA), Inc., for "I wake up every day with..." from A LOTUS GROWS IN THE MUD by Goldie Hawn. Copyright © 2005 by Illume, LLC. All rights reserved.

Nancye Sims for "Leave Good Footprints." Copyright © 2008 by Nancye Sims. All rights reserved.

A careful effort has been made to trace the ownership of selections used in this anthology in order to obtain permission to reprint copyrighted material and give proper credit to the copyright owners. If any error or omission has occurred, it is completely inadvertent, and we would like to make corrections in future editions provided that written notification is made to the publisher:

BLUE MOUNTAIN ARTS, INC., P.O. Box 4549, Boulder, Colorado 80306.